THE NBA

A HISTORY OF HOOPS

Published by Creative Education
P.O. Box 227, Mankato, Minnesota 56002
Creative Education is an imprint of The Creative Company
www.thecreativecompany.us

Design and production by Christine Vanderbeek
Art direction by Rita Marshall

Printed by Corporate Graphics in the United States of America

Photographs by Corbis (Bettmann), Dreamstime (Munktcu), Getty Images
(Glen Allison, Andrew D. Bernstein/NBAE, Scott Cunningham/NBAE, Allen
Einstein/NBAE, Focus on Sport, George Gojkovich, Andy Hayt/NBAE, Glenn
James/NBAE, David E. Klutho/Sports Illustrated, George Long/Sports Illustrated,
Melissa Majchrzak/NBAE, Manny Millan/Sports Illustrated, NBA Photos/NBAE,
NBAE Photos/NBAE, Spencer Platt, Dick Raphael/NBAE, Ezra O. Shaw/Allsport,
SM/AIUEO, Jerry Wachter/Sports Illustrated), iStockphoto (Brandon Laufenberg)

Library of Congress Cataloging-in-Publication Data
Caffrey, Scott.
The story of the Detroit Pistons / by Scott Caffrey.
p. cm. — (The NBA: a history of hoops)
Includes index.
Summary: The history of the Detroit Pistons professional
basketball team from its start in Fort Wayne, Indiana, in 1941 to
today, spotlighting the franchise's greatest players and moments.
ISBN 978-1-58341-943-4
1. Detroit Pistons (Basketball team)—History—Juvenile literature.
I. Title. II. Series.
GV885.52.D47C34 2010   796.323'640977434—dc22   2009035024

CPSIA: 120109 PO1093

First Edition
2 4 6 8 9 7 5 3 1

Page 3: Guard Joe Dumars
Pages 4–5: Guard Will Bynum

THE STORY OF THE

DETROIT

PISTONS

SCOTT CAFFREY

CREATIVE EDUCATION

CONTENTS

CHAPTER ONE

GETTING THE PISTONS PUMPING

Detroit, Michigan, started out as a small French fort in 1701. It was a key site for fur trading, and French and British armies fought many battles with American Indian tribes to gain control of it. Today, Detroit is known as the "Motor City" because it is the home of several American car manufacturers, including Ford, General Motors, and Chrysler. Its automotive history also inspired another nickname—but this one for the musical style that began there, which is known as "Motown."

No matter what people call it, Detroit has a proven record of supporting professional sports teams, too. Since 1957, the city has been home to the Pistons, a franchise in the National Basketball Association (NBA). Given Detroit's business in building cars and car parts, the name was a perfect, albeit coincidental, fit. The team was founded 16 years earlier in Fort Wayne, Indiana, as a member of the National Basketball League (NBL).

The headquarters of General Motors and other titans of America's auto industry, Detroit has built a reputation as a hardworking metropolis.

The club was originally called the Fort Wayne Zollner Pistons in reference to owner Fred Zollner's automotive piston manufacturing company, and its first arena was a high school gym. The Pistons quickly became the NBL's top team, racking up a 101–32 record on their way to four straight division titles (1943 to 1946) and two league championships (1944 and 1945).

The Pistons' first star was guard Bob McDermott, the team's leading scorer in each of its first five seasons. McDermott was known as a player who could score from anywhere on the court, and he also acted as the team's coach. In 1945, after he helped the Pistons rally from a two-games-to-none deficit to beat the Sheboygan Redskins in three straight games to win the championship series, NBL coaches voted McDermott the best player in league history.

COURTSIDE STORIES

THE FLYING Z

The 1945 Fort Wayne team.

IN THE 1930S, FRED ZOLLNER WAS A PROSPEROUS PISTON MANUFACTURER IN FORT WAYNE, INDIANA.

When he founded the Pistons in 1941, "Z" personally scouted his players and made sure to take a hands-on approach with them. He also ensured they received the highest pay in the league. Then, in 1952, when general manager Carl Bennett suggested they fly the team back and forth to away games (instead of taking a bus), Zollner decided to just buy a team airplane. The DC-3 jet was fondly dubbed "The Flying Z" and was outfitted with comfortable furniture, a well-stocked bar, and booster rockets to help the plane lift off in less time. The Fort Wayne Zollner Pistons became the envy of their opponents and rival owners. Bennett, however, recalled that Zollner saw the plane differently. "The funny thing about the plane was that Fred was not a flier," he said. "I mean, he was a real 'white-knuckler' when it came to flying." Zollner may have feared flying, but he was a risk-taker who revolutionized professional basketball and was a key figure in the formation of the NBA in 1949.

LOOKS CAN BE DECEIVING. BY ALL ACCOUNTS, FORWARD GEORGE "BIRD" YARDLEY DIDN'T SEEM TO HAVE THE MAKINGS OF A STAR BASKETBALL PLAYER. But his gangly appearance hid the fact that he was one of the top players of his era. As one of six holdovers from the Fort Wayne squad in 1957, he became Detroit's first team captain. That year, the jump-shot pioneer also turned in a Hall of Fame performance when he set the team record for points scored in one game with 52 against the Syracuse Nationals. His 49 points in a late-season game against the Minneapolis Lakers broke Lakers great George Mikan's NBA season scoring record of 1,932. And in the regular-season finale, Yardley foiled Syracuse's triple-teaming tactics and on his final basket became the first player ever to score 2,000 points in a season—ending with 2,001. "I've been around basketball just about all my life, and I've yet to see a jump shot better than Yardley's," Pistons coach Charley Eckman said. Yardley's Pistons career ended unceremoniously in 1959 after an argument with owner Fred Zollner. He was traded to Syracuse with 15 games left in the season.

n 1948, the Pistons and three other NBL teams were absorbed into the Basketball Association of America (BAA). A year later, the NBL and BAA merged to form the NBA. Zollner played a key role in brokering the league merger, which, as legend has it, took place at his kitchen table. The league shift didn't do the Pistons any favors, though. From 1949 to 1954, Fort Wayne finished no higher than third place in its division and never made it past the second round of the playoffs. But the Pistons did make history on November 22, 1950, by defeating the Minneapolis Lakers 19–18 in the lowest-scoring NBA game ever.

In 1954, Zollner became the first—and still only—team owner to hire a former referee as head coach when he picked Charley Eckman to guide a talented team led by star forward George Yardley, center Larry Foust, and playmaking guard Andy Phillip. In Eckman's first season, the Pistons won the Western Division with a 43–29 record. But they lost to the Syracuse Nationals in the seven-game NBA Finals, blowing a 17-point lead in the first half of Game 7 and eventually losing by just one free throw. The Pistons returned to the Finals in 1956 but were beaten four games to one by the Philadelphia Warriors.

By 1957, Zollner didn't think that the Pistons could compete for much longer in such a small city. "I feel a club can do better in a metropolitan

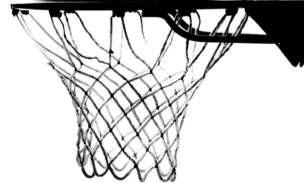

area of 2 million people than an area of 200,000," he said. News of Zollner's impending move cost the club its support, and only 2,212 fans witnessed the team's final game, a playoff loss to the Lakers in March.

Eckman didn't last long once the franchise moved to Detroit. After the Pistons got off to a 9–16 start, Zollner replaced him with former center/forward Ephraim "Red" Rocha. Rocha bolstered the team with some solid talent by trading with the New York Knicks for veterans such as forward Harry Gallatin, center Nat "Sweetwater" Clifton, and guards Dick McGuire and Dick Atha. The best deal, however, was the acquisition of seven-foot center Walter Dukes, a former Harlem Globetrotter who came to the Pistons from Minneapolis in an early-season trade for Foust. Dukes would play 6 seasons in Detroit and retire in 1963 as the team's all-time rebounding king with 4,986 boards (grabbing 6,233 total in his NBA career).

In 1959–60, McGuire was elevated to player/coach status. Rookie forward Bailey Howell joined a loaded roster that won seven of nine games early in the season but eventually ran out of gas. The temporary surge did foreshadow coming success, though. Guard Gene Shue emerged as the team's scoring leader, making the All-Star team, an honor that also went to Dukes and guard Chuck Noble.

n training camp before the 1960–61 season, general manager Nick Kerbawy assessed the team's chances. "We feel [Bob] Ferry, Bailey Howell, and [top draft pick] Jackie Moreland will give us one of the youngest and most promising front lines in NBA history," Kerbawy declared. Howell turned in an impressive season, but the Pistons sputtered and finished just one game out of the Western Division cellar.

Gene Shue was an All-Star in each of his 5 Pistons seasons, and he later earned fame with a successful 22-year NBA coaching career.

BUILDING THE ENGINE

Even though the Pistons had made it to the playoffs every year since moving to Detroit, they had not won a series since their first postseason in Michigan. But a move into Cobo Arena in time for the 1961–62 season got the Pistons pumping again. They dispatched the Cincinnati Royals in the first round of the Western Division playoffs and then went head-to-head with the Los Angeles Lakers in the second round. The two teams battled in a series filled with shifts in momentum, but Detroit couldn't keep up and eventually fell in six games to Los Angeles.

Coach Charles Wolf took over in 1963–64, and the team limped to 23–57. Things got worse when the Pistons opened the next season 2–9. So, on the 12th game of the season, forward Dave DeBusschere took over as player/coach. At the age of 24, DeBusschere became the youngest coach in league history. But he, too, seemed powerless to make his team better, and Detroit dropped to 22–58 in his first full

Dave DeBusschere was a sensational athlete, even beyond basketball; in 1962 and 1963, he pitched for pro baseball's Chicago White Sox.

season as coach. Finally, in 1966–67, with the Pistons mired in last place and only eight games remaining, DeBusschere was replaced by assistant coach Donnis "Donnie" Butcher, a former player who had become the team's top scout.

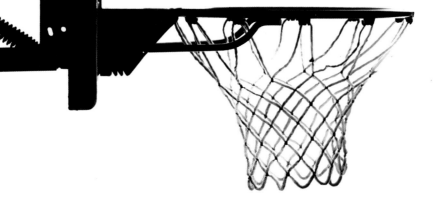

With DeBusschere able to concentrate solely on playing, he worked with guard Dave Bing to bring the team a new sense of hope. In his first season (1966–67), Bing had scored 20 points per game and earned the NBA Rookie of the Year award. "You can't open up a man's chest and look at his heart, but I guarantee there's one big [heart] beating in Bing," said legendary Boston Celtics coach Red Auerbach. "Give me one man like Dave Bing, and I'll build a championship team around him." Unfortunately, the Pistons were never able to do that. Detroit made the 1968 playoffs but struggled the next year when DeBusschere was traded to the Knicks.

With the first pick in the 1970 NBA Draft, Detroit selected a young center named Bob Lanier. At 6-foot-11 and a muscular 250 pounds, Lanier was a powerful specimen. "I was well aware of Bob's great strength," said Cleveland Cavaliers center Steve Patterson after battling

WHEN DAVE BING ARRIVED IN DETROIT IN 1966, HE WAS BILLED AS A BASKETBALL SAVIOR, BUT FANS WERE SKEPTICAL. After all, Bing was the consolation prize in a draft-day coin-flip loss to the New York Knicks that determined which team selected first. But after earning Rookie of the Year honors and then averaging 27.1 points per game during his sophomore season, Bing became a sensation. Upon his retirement from basketball, Bing founded a company that supplied steel to the auto industry—and created the perfect metaphor for his career in the process. Bing was as tough as steel, especially in 1972, when he overcame a career-threatening detached retina that required six hours of surgery. "I went 12 hours without sight," Bing said. "My wife and a friend had to lead me around by the hand." Bing's eyesight never fully recovered, and he had to identify his teammates by their size and uniform. In 1974, he was awarded the NBA's Maurice Stokes Award for his tenacity. Bing remained one of the team's steeliest players, missing only four games over his final three seasons in Detroit. In 2009, he was elected mayor of the city.

INTRODUCING...

BOB LANIER

POSITION CENTER
HEIGHT 6-FOOT-11
PISTONS SEASONS 1970–80

BOB LANIER BEGAN HIS PROFESSIONAL BASKET-BALL CAREER WHILE HE WAS LITERALLY LYING FLAT ON HIS BACK. The Pistons considered Lanier so good that they signed him to a contract as he was laid up on a hospital bed recovering from knee surgery. (He had injured himself while playing in the 1970 college national tournament for St. Bonaventure University.) Lanier possessed a deadly combination of skill and strength. He also happened to have huge feet. His size-22 basketball shoes were the biggest in the league at the time. They were so unique that the Basketball Hall of Fame still features an exhibit where visitors can compare their shoe size with Lanier's. Despite his imposing size, Lanier had a gentle nature. "I think Bob is a very genuine, caring, sensitive, big man," said Joe Dumars, who later played guard for Detroit. "He's a big man who seems to have a tremendously big heart. He's not just saying things in front of the camera." After his playing days ended in 1984, Lanier went on to work with the NBA's Read to Achieve program.

Lanier for a rebound. "I hammered him, and I practically hung on him. Then, all of a sudden, … he just wrapped his arm around me and threw me to the ground like I was made of straw.… I still don't know how he did it."

Lanier was strong enough to briefly revive the sinking Pistons. In 1973–74, under new coach Ray Scott, Detroit jumped to a 52–30 mark and made the playoffs for the first of four straight seasons. But the team would not be able to sustain the success, and those would be the Pistons' last good seasons for a long time. In 1974, Zollner sold the club to entrepreneur William Davidson with assurances that the Pistons would remain in Michigan forever. Then, in 1975, the team traded Bing to the Washington Bullets.

In 1978, the Pistons became part of the Eastern Conference and were placed in the Central Division. Lanier was traded to the Milwaukee Bucks in the middle of the 1979–80 season. Without the big center in the middle, Detroit plunged to 16–66 and found itself in desperate need of a hero.

Guard Eric Money, who was only 19 years old when he joined the Pistons, was a bright spot for Detroit during some mediocre mid-'70s seasons.

That hero arrived via the second overall pick in the 1981 NBA Draft: point guard Isiah Thomas, who had just led Indiana University to the national collegiate championship. "I believe God made people to perform certain acts," said Will Robinson, Detroit's assistant general manager. "Frank Sinatra was made to sing, Jesse Owens was made to run, and Isiah Thomas was made to play basketball."

Another 1981 draft pick, Kelly Tripucka, was a high-scoring forward from Notre Dame who also showed promise. During the 1981–82 season, the Pistons traded with the Seattle SuperSonics to obtain proven veteran guard Vinnie Johnson, a proficient scorer who was an effective outside shooter but also strong enough to muscle his way past bigger players on the inside. Late in that season, Detroit traded with its rival, Cleveland, for tough-guy center Bill Laimbeer. And finally, the Pistons hired Chuck Daly as their head coach in 1983. The championship pieces were finally starting to fall into place.

Although average at best defensively, Kelly Tripucka could score with the best of them, netting 26.5 points a game in his second NBA season.

CHAPTER THREE

BACK-TO-BACK CHAMPIONS

Detroit's play improved quickly, and the Pistons made it to the second round of the 1985 Eastern Conference playoffs against the Boston Celtics. In Game 4 of that series, Johnson earned a lasting nickname. After Johnson had wowed Pistons fans by scoring 22 fourth-quarter points in a 102–99 win over Boston to tie the series, Celtics guard Danny Ainge remarked, "If that guy in Chicago [football player William Perry] is 'The Refrigerator,' then Vinnie Johnson is 'The Microwave.' He sure heated up in a hurry." But Boston bested Detroit in each of the remaining two games.

In 1985, more pieces of the Pistons' rebuilding project fell into place. In the NBA Draft that year, they selected a little-known guard from McNeese State University named Joe Dumars. Most Pistons fans were angry that the team had passed on local favorite Sam Vincent, a high-scoring Michigan State University standout. But with three excellent point guards already—Thomas, Johnson, and John Long—Detroit felt it could take a chance on this hidden gem of a player.

Even though Vinnie Johnson was primarily a bench player, he was so valuable to Detroit that the team retired his jersey number in 1994.

The team also traded with the Bullets for forwards Rick Mahorn and Mike Gibson. The next year, Detroit drafted 6-foot-11 center John Salley from the Georgia Institute of Technology and a wily forward from tiny Southeastern Oklahoma State University named Dennis Rodman. Before the 1986–87 season began, the team also added another impressive player when it shipped Tripucka to the Utah Jazz for Adrian Dantley, one of the best-scoring small forwards and toughest low-post threats in the league. Detroit was now loaded with talent.

A formidable shot blocker, center John Salley also helped the Pistons by keeping the team loose with his lively, comedic personality.

INTRODUCING...
CHUCK DALY

COACH
PISTONS SEASONS 1983–92

EVER SINCE HIS CHILDHOOD IN PENNSYLVANIA, CHUCK DALY HAD LOVED EVERYTHING ABOUT BASKETBALL. He never forgot the white leather basketball he and his brother Bud had received when Chuck was 12. "When you don't have much materially in life and suddenly you own such a treasure, you think you've died and gone to heaven," Daly said. "I couldn't believe it. Nobody in the world had a white basketball except the Daly brothers." Such appreciation helped Daly bring an intense passion to his teams, especially to Detroit's champion "Bad Boys" crew. "Chuck Daly was the perfect coach for us," guard Isiah Thomas said. "He realized this team was something special, and it seemed as if he pressed the right buttons." Pressing buttons became a Pistons trademark, as Daly's squads played aggressively and often angered opponents along the way. Chicago Bulls star Michael Jordan called them the "dirtiest team in basketball." But Daly knew he coached a special team. "Teams win championships, not individuals," he said. "The players must have the ability.... They have to be unselfish, and it's hard to find unselfish players."

DURING THE 1980S, WHEN THE DETROIT PISTONS WERE KNOWN AS THE "BAD BOYS," CENTER BILL LAIMBEER WAS CONSIDERED THE WORST OF THEM ALL. He threw elbows, fists, and hips into his opponents and probably earned more boos and vile nicknames from opposing fans than anyone in the history of the NBA. Opposing players often retaliated with punches, for, as Boston Celtics forward Larry Bird once said, "We don't like him that good." Eventually, the Chicago Bulls decided to try and get to the bottom of Laimbeer's tactics. They trained a camera on Laimbeer throughout the 1991 playoffs to see what he was doing. What they discovered was amazing–Laimbeer often grabbed players at their pressure points (such as on the biceps or a nerve on the forearm) to deaden their arms. Chicago formally complained to the league, but no action was taken. Through it all, Laimbeer was a four-time All-Star who helped the Pistons win a pair of championships. He also became the 19th player in NBA history to collect more than 10,000 career points (with 13,790) and 10,000 rebounds (with 10,400).

INTENSE PRESSURE

Bill Laimbeer elbows Larry Bird as they fight for a rebound.

C oach Daly preached an aggressive defense, and the Pistons earned the nickname "Bad Boys" for their physical style of play. Thomas directed the offense and became an incomparable floor general. Dumars and Johnson were an interchangeable rotation at the other guard position. Laimbeer and Mahorn proved to be imposing enforcers and shot blockers in the paint, while Dantley was a nightmare for defenders in the half-court. Salley and Rodman, meanwhile, provided sparks off the bench by disrupting their opponents' rhythms with tough, smothering defense and efficient rebounding. Rodman in particular was relentless, becoming known as "Worm" for his ability to squirm between players underneath the basket and snag rebounds. The Pistons soared to a 52–30 mark and reached the 1987 Eastern Conference finals, where they fell to the Celtics.

ISIAH "ZEKE" THOMAS SPENT HIS ENTIRE PLAYING CAREER IN DETROIT AND WAS THE UNQUESTIONED LEADER OF THE "BAD BOYS." "If I'm just trying to sum Zeke up in a couple of sentences, it's almost impossible to do," teammate Joe Dumars said. "By far, he's the best player I've ever played with." After the Pistons finally broke out of their playoff rut and reached the 1988 NBA Finals, they took a three-games-to-two series lead over the Los Angeles Lakers. But in the third quarter of Game 6, Thomas sprained his ankle. Yet the injury seemed to make him stronger and more determined. By the end of the quarter, he had scored 25 points, an NBA Finals record for a single quarter. But Thomas's 43 total points weren't enough, and the Pistons then lost the series when he was unable to contribute much in Game 7. Thomas took the loss to heart and worked even harder to help the Pistons become the league's best team, and as a result, they won back-to-back championships. Upon retirement, Thomas entered the executive ranks with the Toronto Raptors and the New York Knicks.

etroit stormed back the next season, winning both the division and the conference, something it had not done since the 1950s. In the six-game conference finals, the Pistons demolished the Celtics, who won by the narrowest of margins in their two victories. At long last, Detroit was in the NBA Finals. Although the Pistons lost to the Lakers in seven hard-fought games, they would not be denied the next season.

In 1988–89, the team moved into a new arena, The Palace of Auburn Hills. That season, the Pistons dominated the league with a 63–19 record and pounded their way through the playoffs to meet the Lakers again in the Finals. This rematch was no contest as Detroit swept L.A. in four games, thanks largely to the hot shooting of Dumars. The versatile guard exploded for an average of 27.3 points per game during the series and was named Finals Most Valuable Player (MVP). "Dumars wouldn't miss," said Mitch Kupchak, a Lakers team official. "We kept waiting for him to miss. You could feel the whole building waiting. But it was as if he had forgotten how."

The Pistons roared to a third consecutive division title the next season and once again reached the Finals, where they battled star guard Clyde Drexler and the Portland Trail Blazers. The five-game series turned out to be a lopsided affair, with Portland's sole victory coming in overtime of Game 2. Thomas was masterful in the series. To observers, it seemed

Dennis Rodman spent part of the 1989 Finals defending center Kareem Abdul-Jabbar and part defending guard Magic Johnson (pictured).

he was all over the court, making shot after shot and doing a little bit of everything to help the Pistons win. For his efforts, he was voted Finals MVP after averaging 27.6 points, 7 assists, and 5.2 rebounds per game. In Game 5, Johnson lived up to his clutch reputation as "The Microwave" when he nailed the unforgettable series-winning shot with 0.7 seconds remaining.

The Pistons were back-to-back champions, and they were eager to "three-peat." But it was not to be. In the 1991 playoffs, superstar guard Michael Jordan and the Bulls—whom the Pistons had repeatedly beaten in previous years' playoffs—finally won the conference, effectively replacing Detroit as the top Eastern heavyweight. In 1992–93, the Pistons went 40–42 and missed the playoffs for the first time in a decade, even while maintaining their main core of players. After that, Rodman was traded to the San Antonio Spurs, and Laimbeer and Thomas retired. By 1994, only the ageless Dumars remained from Detroit's championship era.

JOE DUMARS

POSITION GUARD
HEIGHT 6-FOOT-3
PISTONS SEASONS 1985–99

EVEN THOUGH MANY DETROIT FANS HAD NEVER HEARD OF JOE DUMARS WHEN HE WAS DRAFTED, DUMARS'S HARDWORKING STYLE OF PLAY QUICKLY ENDEARED HIM TO THE PISTONS FAITHFUL. Dumars was considered one of the greatest competitors in the league and was so widely respected that he was awarded the inaugural NBA Sportsmanship Award in 1996. Thereafter, the league even named the award's trophy after him. By the time his playing days ended in 1999, Dumars had become the team's leading three-point shooter, with 990 made, and its second-leading scorer, with 16,401 career points. "Throughout his 14-year career, Joe carried himself with dignity and integrity and showed that one can be both a great athlete and a great sportsman," league deputy commissioner Russ Granik said on the occasion of Dumars's retirement. The Pistons didn't allow Dumars to go far from them, though. He was immediately hired as president of Detroit's basketball operations and excelled at that, too. As the architect of Detroit's remarkable two-year turnaround in 2001 and 2002, he was named by *The Sporting News* as NBA Executive of the Year in 2003.

CHAPTER FOUR

PISTONS STEAL A CROWN

Detroit began rebuilding when it selected forward Grant Hill in the 1994 NBA Draft and paired him with young sharp-shooting guard Allan Houston. Although Detroit's record was only 28–54 that year, Hill became the first Pistons player since Dave Bing to be named Rookie of the Year (an honor Hill shared with Dallas Mavericks point guard Jason Kidd).

Under new coach Doug Collins, the 1995–96 Pistons leapt to 46–36. Although they made the playoffs, they were swept by the Orlando Magic. Then, in 1997, they brought in two key additions when they traded for guard/forward Jerry Stackhouse and signed center Brian Williams (who later changed his name to Bison Dele). That year, Hill became the first player since Celtics great Larry Bird (in 1989–90) to average at least 20 points, 9 rebounds, and 7 assists per game in a season, an accomplishment that has not been duplicated since.

Although it seemed as if Dumars could play forever, he finally retired in 1999 and became the team's president. He left a huge hole in the lineup, and the team struggled for wins. Despite Hill's statistical supremacy, Detroit never advanced far

Grant Hill spent his six finest seasons in Detroit; after he left the Pistons in 2000, the remainder of his career was undercut by injuries.

in the playoffs. So, in 2000, when Hill opted to become a free agent, the Pistons organized a sign-and-trade deal with Orlando. In return for Hill, they received guard Chucky Atkins plus Ben Wallace, an intimidating 6-foot-9 center with rippling muscles and a fuzzy Afro, who would go on to win four NBA Defensive Player of the Year trophies in Detroit.

Rick Carlisle was named head coach in 2001 and soon jump-started the Pistons. In two seasons under Carlisle, Detroit finished 50–32 and charged deep into the playoffs. In 2002, the Pistons traded for smooth-scoring guard Richard Hamilton, who worked alongside do-it-all rookie forward Tayshaun Prince. But even though he had brought competitive basketball back to the Motor City, Carlisle was let go in 2003 after the Pistons were swept by the New Jersey Nets in the Eastern Conference finals.

The Pistons then made headlines by signing Hall of Fame coach Larry Brown away from the Philadelphia 76ers. Brown was determined to make Detroit a winner again. "I saw a team with a chance to win, a team with quality ownership in Mr. [William] Davidson and quality leadership with a guy like Joe [Dumars], a team with character guys," Brown said upon arriving in Detroit.

COURTSIDE STORIES

THE DELE MYSTERY

Bison Dele at the free-throw line.

FORMERLY NAMED BRIAN WILLIAMS, CENTER BISON DELE WAS WELL KNOWN FOR HIS ECCENTRICITIES. As the son of Eugene Williams from the 1950s singing group The Platters, Dele was also an accomplished bass guitar player. But to basketball, Dele brought a sweet left-handed shot and a championship pedigree from the Chicago Bulls to the Pistons for two seasons in the late 1990s. However, he suddenly retired at age 30 in the prime of his career. Three years later, in July 2002, when Dele's brother, Miles Dabord, docked Dele's catamaran at a port in the Tahitian capital of Papeete, the suspicions of authorities were aroused. Dele, his girlfriend, a skipper, and Dabord had all been traveling on the boat, but only Dabord returned. So what happened to Dele? Nobody knows for sure. Dabord, the main suspect and the only witness, died two months later and was never interviewed. Some say Dele's boat was hijacked by pirates, but most assume that he and his girlfriend were killed and thrown overboard by Dabord, who was known to have used his brother's identity to obtain money.

INTRODUCING...

RICHARD HAMILTON

POSITION GUARD / FORWARD
HEIGHT 6-FOOT-6
PISTONS SEASONS 2002–PRESENT

AS A HIGH-SCHOOLER IN THE MINING TOWN OF COATESVILLE, PENNSYLVANIA, RICHARD HAMILTON DEVELOPED INTO A LOCAL BASKETBALL LEGEND. Although he did not make the varsity team his freshman year, he did catch the eye of coach Ricky Hicks, who took him under his wing. Hamilton met with Hicks most mornings at six o'clock to work on his game. Hicks also taught him a unique breathing technique that

afforded Hamilton better stamina. It was around this time that Hamilton first learned of another basketball phenom from eastern Pennsylvania named Kobe Bryant. During a three-on-three tournament in Philadelphia, Bryant's father, Joe, was watching the action and couldn't help but notice Hamilton, because he was the only other player who could keep up with his son. Hamilton and Bryant would face off throughout high

school and even play together on state all-star teams. Once he reached the pros, "Rip" solidified his status as one of the league's most talented stars, exhibiting a sweet mid-range jumper on offense and playing relentless defense on the other end. Hamilton separated himself to become the Pistons' clear leader in the mid-2000s.

The Pistons started the 2003–04 season well, but a late-season trade for power forward Rasheed Wallace kicked Hamilton, Ben Wallace, point guard Chauncey Billups, and the rest of the team into high gear. They finished 54–28 and raced through the playoffs to meet the Lakers in the NBA Finals. Despite all of his individual achievements, Ben Wallace, for one, considered reaching the Finals his finest honor. "Yeah, [winning awards] means a lot, but it is not something I am going to hang my hat on," he said. "Winning the Finals is our main focus."

The star-laden Lakers were fresh off three consecutive NBA championships from 2000 through 2002. But the Pistons shocked the sports world by beating the Lakers four games to one for the franchise's third league championship. "We didn't worry about what people wrote in the papers or what people were saying on TV," said Hamilton. "We said to ourselves, 'Anything is possible if you play together as five, not just on the offensive end but on the defensive end, too.'"

BASKET-BRAWL AT THE PALACE

A referee tries to separate Ben Wallace and Ron Artest.

WHEN THE DETROIT PISTONS TOOK ON THE INDIANA PACERS ON NOVEMBER 19, 2004, AT THE PALACE OF AUBURN HILLS, NO ONE EXPECTED A BOXING MATCH TO ENSUE. But in this game, basketball took a back seat to punching. The problem started with a scuffle between Pistons center Ben Wallace and Pacers forward Ron Artest. Things escalated from there. Officials stopped the game with 45.9 seconds remaining after players from both teams joined in the pushing and shoving. As Artest rested on the scorer's table after he was separated from the fray, a Pistons fan lobbed a drink that struck him. Artest and Pacers forward Stephen Jackson jumped into the crowd, and as other Indiana players joined them, players and fans exchanged punches, while ice, cups, and other debris rained down onto the court, and a full-on riot ensued. After the brawl, many players were fined and suspended, and some fans were even prosecuted in court for various assault charges. Said NBA commissioner David Stern, "The events of the game were shocking, repulsive, and inexcusable, a humiliation for everyone associated with the NBA."

GUARD LINDSEY HUNTER TOOK A CIRCUITOUS ROUTE TO CHAMPIONSHIP GLORY WITH THE PISTONS. He spent the first seven years of his career in Detroit but was traded in 2000 to the Milwaukee Bucks. Milwaukee then shipped him to Los Angeles, where he was a contributor to the Lakers' 2002 NBA championship run. Los Angeles then moved him to the Toronto Raptors, who eventually shuffled him back to Detroit before the 2003–04 season. The Pistons stashed him on the injured list, then on the bench, and eventually traded him to the Celtics, who released him a week later without ever putting him into a game. Hunter then made his way back to Detroit. "I really believe all things happen for a reason," Hunter said. "And the reason all this has happened to me this season is ... I don't know that yet.... I know I can make a good contribution, and we're getting ready to win the NBA title." Indeed, Hunter returned just in time to help the Pistons win the 2004 NBA championship against the Lakers.

COURTSIDE STORIES

LINDSEY HUNTER'S ODYSSEY

Lindsey Hunter scores a layup.

n 2004–05, the Pistons nearly pulled off a repeat, making it all the way to the Finals before the Spurs beat them in seven games. Detroit seemed destined for another Finals appearance the following year after barreling to a franchise-best 64–18 record under new coach Flip Saunders. But the team fell apart in the conference finals and lost to the Miami Heat. Still, the Pistons had accomplished much in just a few seasons. "We got to the Finals twice and won it once," said Billups. "I think that is a great run."

Detroit remained formidable over the next few seasons as it marched to the Eastern Conference finals twice more. In 2007, the Pistons lost in the conference finals to forward LeBron James and his upstart crew of Cleveland Cavaliers. And in 2007–08, Detroit got some spark from young-gun players such as forward Jason Maxiell and guard Rodney Stuckey, but the team lost out to the loaded Celtics in the conference finals and watched as Boston won the NBA championship. In 2008–09, the Pistons made a move that damaged the team's chemistry, trading

Billups to the Denver Nuggets for veteran guard Allen Iverson. Detroit missed the playoffs for the first time in eight years, then slid down the Central Division standings the next year, despite the best efforts of Hamilton, Stuckey, and young forward Jonas Jerebko.

The Pistons have always made their fans proud with their tough style of play, whether it was as the Bad Boys of the 1980s or the crew of defensive stalwarts that propelled the Pistons to a championship in 2004. With the continued backing of the Detroit faithful, the Pistons will definitely keep their motor running high in search of their next championship.

Detroit struggled in 2009–10, despite the aggressive scoring of Rodney Stuckey (opposite) and the versatility of Tayshaun Prince (below).

INDEX